Mommy Millionaire Success Habits:

Simple Routines That Will Help Moms Reach Their Life Goals

By Anna Harrison

Description

This book will teach you as a mom how to build a strong belief in yourself, your abilities, and your dreams. Then you'll get help to convert your goals and ambitions into a set of targets.

You will also learn how to rid yourself of any negative, self-defeating fears, habits, and beliefs that may be keeping you from moving forward. While it is important to know what to do, you need to understand how you can do it.

For you as a mom, this book will teach you how to develop a positive attitude toward your financial expenses and how you can save money now. Poor people with bad money management skills can win the lottery, but those same choices and attitudes toward money have time and again led to lottery winners ending up broke again in a few years.

This phenomenon is also observable in the sports and entertainment industries where people are catapulted to stardom, but have such low money IQ they end up broke within years.

As a mother, you can create the wealth you have always dreamt about if you take actions armed with the right information. Positive thinking is only the first step in creating success; you must learn how to put what you visualize into practice to achieve results, and this book will teach you just that.

Table of Contents

Description
Introduction
Chapter 1: Money and Happiness
Chapter 2: What to do and Avoid When Developing New Habits
Chapter 3: Money Mindset
Chapter 4: Build a Reserve but Don't Hoard It
Chapter 5: Habits You Should Change in the Next 24 hours
Chapter 6: Time Management
Chapter 7: Kids and Money
Chapter 8: Budgeting Goals Accountability
Conclusion

Introduction

This book focuses on what makes millionaires financially successful. This book will show you how you too can be a Mommy millionaire by chronicling how they think and act. Our repetitive thoughts and actions are what become our habits. We will also look at a few practical ideas that can be adapted, whether you have just started your millionaire journey or are looking to expedite your success. In this book, you will learn what you need to become successful in almost any field.

Success is like a game with a predetermined set of rules you must learn to become a winner. But how can you win if you don't know what the rules are?

People can seem like they are winning without having taken time out to learn the rules, but they will often end up back at the start because they failed to understand the principles needed to be financially successful in life. Have you ever wondered why you keep earning more and more wages yet you still are not able to make ends meet? Chances are you have not learned to play the game.

The basics of all the principles in this book apply to everyone regardless of where you fit on the ladder of success. Whether you aim to be the best sales representative at your place of work, you want to save and buy a house, or you simply wish to become wealthy, these principles are designed for you. You need to understand, own, and apply them with a lot of discipline, and they will change your life along with how your peers see you. You must realize, however, that you will need to work hard while at the same time practicing what you learn in this book to achieve success.

Chapter 1: Money and Happiness

As has been argued, the link between happiness and money exists, but conditionally. The requisite condition for triggering happiness arising from making and having money is personal financial management. It is while preparing a financial plan that one can further add a social philosophy to money to humanize it. Well-managed money will enable one to afford material resources needed to make life comfortable and help create room for other social and familial engagement that can elicit happiness. The truth is that significant time is spent sourcing money or repaying the money at the expense of the family. Extended work can harm the personal connection between family members. In this manner, having a personal budget equals addressing one of the root causes of familial disputes and disconnections.

I know you have heard conflicting statements and theories about the link of money and happiness or lack of happiness. We will take the argument that money can be a source of happiness. Money is a resource and not the happiness itself, and perhaps this is what creates confusion. Let us take a simple example of water. For all people, water is a resource and it depends on how we use water to get value out of it. For instance, one may use water for swimming, for laundry, for cleaning, and as a water fountain. Another person might decide to let the water run, consuming everything in the house with wetness and, in this case, making water a great source of distress. The same is true with money; it all depends on an individual's discipline, goals, and management.

For one to survive, especially in the contemporary world, we need resources. We need services. For us to feel comfortable, we need to have electricity, gas for our vehicles, water, and active health insurance. We cannot be happy if we are not comfortable first. While an individual may experience short-term happiness without all these resources, with time, that person will have to look for a portion of these resources to induce happiness again. Additionally, we are now living in a formalized economy where the concept of a person being self-sufficient is fast waning. The implication of all this is that we cannot produce all we need, and this means we have to frequently source some services and materials for our living.

Expectedly, this is where the criticality of money as an enabler to acquire resources surfaces. By having a requisite amount of money, we can acquire and pay for transport, electricity, and water. With an adequate amount of money, we can access high-quality healthcare and fix our aching bodies. Money is necessary for one to acquire needed resources as mentioned. However, since money is a resource, it means that its supply is limited and we must have a way of ensuring that we spend this resource prudently. Just like any other resource, like oil, we need to consistently monitor and manage acquisition, usage, and saving money for the future.

If there is both a plan and financial management in place, then the link between money and happiness will exist. By having a good personal budget or family budget, a family will be able to conveniently afford primary needs such as education, healthcare, food, and clothing. The family may also be able to afford holidays and other recreational needs. It can then be argued that when family stresses and worries are minimized or eliminated, they will have adequate time to explore other critical areas of life. As an illustration, a couple will spend quality time at home discussing the progress and future of their children, devoid of incessant complaints and emotional breakdowns. By having time and resources to focus on children, the children may be cushioned against poor parenting outcomes such as excess drinking leading to alcoholism. All these illustrations suggest that the link between money and happiness exist, but conditionally.

While there are numerous inputs to attain happiness, affordability and acquisition of basic resources is necessary for achieving happiness. It is not possible for you to be happy when you cannot afford rent, pay for electricity, and occasionally afford a simple holiday. The argument here is that money is not happiness, but money is the greatest enabler of happiness. Therefore, with a good financial plan that allows balancing of social life and work life or business life, a person has a significant opportunity to not only be happy but also create happiness for those around them.

Finally, money, as a potential source of happiness, is the reward phenomenon of earning or making money. When one accomplishes their individual targets at work or in business, money is a common and acknowledged reward. When a person improves the management of their personal finances, the result is making more savings, which is a great source of feeling not only happiness but also feeling invaluable. We can summarize the attributes of having money that qualify it as an inducer of happiness as being an enabler of acquiring resources, services, and commodities. This is a reward for an individual's efforts and creating a path to move into a comfort zone.

Chapter 2: What to do and Avoid When Developing New Habits

Now, it is time to know exactly what to do to replace bad habits that are inhibiting your level of self-discipline. There are common things to try, and to avoid when you are working on replacing your bad habits. It is important to know what these are so that you are reducing the number of challenges you might face throughout the process.

What to Avoid When Replacing Bad Habits

When you are working to replace a bad habit and change your behavior, it is important to recognize the common mistakes at the outset, because then you can work to prepare for them and minimize any issues as you go about your journey of creating new habits. The following are the most common habit-breaking-and-making mistakes:

Relying Solely on Willpower

Willpower alone is not capable of helping you make and maintain long-term changes. It just is not enough. It can help to get you started, but as a mental and emotional resource, it is a limited one. So, if you have strong willpower, use it to spur the breaking of your habit, but know you will need additional resources to go further.

Creating Only the Ultimate Goal

All reasonable goals are made up of multiple smaller goals that need to be accomplished first, to achieve your ultimate goal. Your ultimate goal of breaking the bad habit needs to be broken down into several small, easier steps that you will plan for and focus on individually.

Ignoring the Impact of Your Environment

Your behavior is dependent on multiple factors, including your environment. To change your behavior, you almost always have to change your environment, whether it means taking yourself out of the environment or changing elements of the environment itself. There is no way around this if you want true success.

Focusing Only on Stopping Bad Habits

Yes, the ultimate goal is ending your bad habit, but you have to replace it with a good one for the process to work. You cannot just end the bad habit and be done. Intentionally put something in its place and focus on the new habit for the long term.

Blaming Your Lack of Motivation

Motivation is one of many emotional states, and like willpower, it is very limited. Life is not predictable, and as things change, so does your motivation. Because of this, you cannot use motivation alone to make long-term and meaningful changes.

Not Focusing on Cues

Remember the cues associated with your habits? You must identify the cues to all the habits you are trying to break. These cues must be changed or eliminated in order for you to be successful in altering the bad habits associated with them. *Thinking* that information causes action. Remember that power comes from both application and knowledge. You have to allow your emotions concerning these habits to influence you to make positive changes. If you only rely on the knowledge that they are bad, you will not succeed.

Focusing on Abstract Goals

Goals are good, and you need them, but you also need a call to action. For example, if your goal is to quit smoking, you cannot just tell yourself to quit. You also need a plan. For example, tell yourself to give up one cigarette per day every four days until you have quit.

Focusing Only on the Future

Creating long-term goals is great and necessary, but you also have to think of the present. When you are looking to change a bad habit, take it a day at a time.

Making Excuses

Any positive change in life can quickly be killed by excuses, so stop making them.

Powerful Methods that Work to Replace Bad Habits

This section will help you to develop the specific strategy to make sure that your bad habits start to fade, and new, constructive ones take their place.

1. Fine yourself.

This is to be taken literally, as you will get a jar and actually put money into it when you fall back into your old bad habits. This makes the act of the habit more painful, and once you finally break free of it, you can use the money that you accumulate to help you improve a good habit. For example, if you are trying to break the habit of overspending by saving more, put this money into your savings.

2. Understand why the habit is bad.

Not all bad habits are obvious. At this point, you need to dig deeper and determine why they are bad, perhaps in how the habit affects your long-term goals. From here, seek out a suitable replacement that is similar in nature to the old habit, but can make a positive impact instead.

3. Use a calendar to track progress.

Every time you utilize a good habit to replace a bad one, you want to keep track of this. Set up a calendar that you will use specifically for this purpose and put an "X" on every day that you succeed. As you see more days marked off, this makes it easier to stay on track.

4. Give yourself time to prepare.

Take a full week just preparing to make the change from a bad habit to a good one. Make a plan and determine exactly which good habit you will use as a replacement, and when.

5. Make a list of positive elements.

Once you determine which positive habit you will use to replace a good one, write down at least five benefits you will get for adopting the good habit.

6. Change your environment.

You read about this in the above section that your environment, if you make no changes, can make it harder to break a habit. Consider what about your environment needs to change to eliminate the old habit and accommodate the positive replacement. Then, immediately start making those changes.

7. Talk to yourself.

When you notice yourself falling back into the bad habit, talk yourself out of it, and verbally explain to yourself why the good habit you are working to develop is in your best interest.

8. Review your relapses.

If you relapse into your bad habit, take a serious and objective review into why it happened. This will help you understand why it occurred, so that you can make a plan to avoid the same pattern in the future.

9. Create a loop.

You want to have a habit loop for your new good habit. Create your cue, routine, and reward. Write this information down so that it is easier to remember, and review as needed.

10. Retrain your mind.

You want to train your mind to see your bad habits as negative and your new good habits as a positive thing. Repetition of these ideas helps ingrain both the mindset and the habit.

Chapter 3: Money Mindset

For centuries, money has been misunderstood. Some people think of it as evil, others think it a savior that can solve all our problems. Neither of these assertions is true. Money, however, exposes man's true heart and true nature.

Our attitude toward money shapes how we think about it and how we behave with money. Money is an inanimate object, but our attitude toward money is what forms the basis for our money habits. The woman who grew up poor can be a millionaire but still think of money as a scarce resource that is limited in supply, and this may cause her to hoard it.

I once heard a friend of mine who happens to be a nurse who cares for senior citizens in their houses, give an account about an old lady who stuffed her pillow and died with several hundred thousand stashed in her mattress. Growing up during a world war had given her a mindset that money was limited and scarce.

Millionaires have learned the adage "Money begets money."

We must look at ourselves and decide what is our mindset in regards to money.

Once you take on a new mindset, you will be surprised by how much money you already have and what you can do with it.

A dear friend of mine complained that money is like water in our palms and will slip away at any given chance. Others believe that they can challenge life and overcome it.

A million dollars is an enormous amount of money to throw away, yet every day many people do just that, throwing away the opportunity to be a millionaire amid the daily financial decisions we all have to make. Without realizing it, they have a negative million-dollar habit. "Hang on," you say, "I never had a million dollars to lose—nor have any of my companions." That is likely genuine, yet consistently, many individuals spend cash on things they don't need. Frequently such spending is just chronic, the morning Starbucks, new accessories, another pair of shoes or dinners out.

One dollar, sufficiently given time and the habit of accumulating funds will develop into a million dollars. By permanently modifying a couple of practices or propensities and contributing the cash that can be spared, anybody can be a mogul in their lifetime. The more you can save, the faster the procedure works.

This procedure is *not* about rationing and saving, nor renouncing life's joys primarily to amass a million dollars at some point later on.

You must develop a millionaire mindset in which you view your cash as an asset that is working to contribute to increasing your long-term wealth. By saving the cash that would somehow be spent on other propensities, it is frequently enough to make a mogul! A woman with savings has options.

Saving Money

Saving money is an arduous task for everyone, as it comprises a strong determination and control over expenses. On the other hand, changing longtime habits is tough as well. But, saving money is not an impossible task when it becomes the goal.

Motivate Yourself with a Goal

Set a strict and realistic goal for a particular span and regularly review them. Cut out pictures of your goal and place them where you will constantly see them in your home, so that every time you see them, you are reminded of the goal. It is important to also remind yourself of the purpose of the goal as it helps to save money easily and stay on course.

Pay Yourself First

By saving a portion of money before investing, you will learn the self-discipline to keep control over excess expenses. It also helps the goal setter to be in control and manage better according to the goal.

Track Unnecessary Expenses

One needs to keep a check over unnecessary expenses, as any negligence will delay and derail your financial objectives. Be strict on the goal and be determined to not spend extra. Excess spending is like holes in the haul of a ship; you need to identify where these leaks are fast and stop the sinking. Once you have plugged all the holes, it will be easier for you to get rid of the water you have taken on that is slowing your success boat down!

Save Spare Change

Get a jar and put all the spare change into it. It is not too time-consuming to do this. Therefore, anyone can do it. Spare cash or change will make a difference at the end of a month. The idea behind this is not that you become a penny pincher, but you train your mind to become more conscious of saving money in the little places you can. I coached one lady, and within months, she started to see savings opportunities everywhere around her. She noticed that by changing her gym, she could save a few hundred every year, and by emptying the junk from the back of the car, she could save on the amount of gas needed for her car. By buying in bulk when there were special deals at the supermarket, she could save hundreds. She said to me, "I wait till toothpaste is half price and buy enough for the year, and I repeat this for as many non-perishable goods as I can." After two years, this lady had enough saved for a deposit on a house and she hasn't looked back, as she now applies the same cost-cutting methods to her real estate and property renovation projects. So the point of this is to claw back as much money as is wasted and put it toward your dream.

Avoid a Quick Decision On an Expensive Purchase

Take the time to think about what to buy and when to buy it. Evaluate the price and need of the good before making any decision to buy or not.

Exchange Tips with Other Savers

Share money-saving tips with those close to you to get better ideas and exchange tips (people may often have saving tips and may be inclined to share with you if you first share yours). You can also get help from money-saving books and websites to motivate you to save more. These books and websites will help to adopt some better ways to save money.

Celebrate the Success

Once you develop the saving habit don't forget to celebrate once in a while. Self-reward boosts your confidence of saving money, and by rewarding yourself, you associate some positivity with your saving habits. Cutting costs and saving may mean for a while you can't impulsively buy things like you used to, but rewarding yourself reinforces in your subconscious mind that your new habits will pay off in the long term. So celebrate in any little way you can and one day you will have the financial power to buy what you want if you stay committed to your habits.

Track Your Spending—Create a Budget

For some individuals, making a spending plan is extremely exhausting and stressful. Be that as it may, the truth of the matter is you can't comprehend what you're spending without having an appropriate spending plan. It is a device that assists you with knowing where your cash is going.

You have to dispense a specific measure of your wage for each necessary expenditure such as sustenance, garments, transportation, stimulation, health, and so forth. Expect that you have planned $2000 for nourishment in a month, and then you have to confine your spending during this length of time to the sum set. Budgeting offers you some assistance with planning before you spend. Consequently, budgeting is a significant stride to spare cash as it permits you to control your spending. Otherwise, you may not know the amount of cash that is being squandered.

Control Spending

Controlling spending does not imply that you have to carry on like a penny pincher. It just means that you ought to spend cash wisely.

Case in point, abstaining from eating out day by day won't just offer you some assistance with controlling spending, additionally it will offer you some assistance with straying far from tough well-being issues. Eating out only on special events with your family would give you a chance to appreciate the sustenance.

Along these lines, restrict your yearnings. Spend cash just when you have sufficiently collected savings for crises and future costs. You must practice self-control if you want to expedite the saving process.

Chapter 4: Build a Reserve but Don't Hoard It

Now that we have a budget that is guiding you, and you have revised it to make sure that expenses do not gobble more than 50% of your income, you should now establish a savings account. Take measures to ensure that the savings account is not linked to your credit cards or phone applications, to minimize the temptation of withdrawing money from the account. By saving in this account each month, you are building a financial reserve. The cash reserve should be built based on the savings goals you set. You should maintain highly disciplined and avoid the temptation to use some of this cash and reimburse later. Not making any withdrawal from this account should be part of your goals or objectives.

Apart from savings accumulated, any other money you make should be kept in this account. For instance, monetary rewards, a pay raise, or bonus payments constitute unplanned income and should be saved. When given a shopping voucher, you should save a similar amount in your bank's savings account. Even with an unexpected financial boost, you should always stick to your personal budget, which is managing expenses and saving as much as possible with acceptable levels of comfort. When you purchase goods on a discount, remember to save that money, and you should not spend the discounted amount on more shopping.

After three months, you will notice your savings account is growing and you might be adjusting to the foregone comforts. It is important to acknowledge that you will feel the temptation to immediately invest the cash saved. It is not yet advisable to immerse yourself in investments, even though there might be alluring offers in the market. The focus should remain saving and building cash reserves. The motivations for saving and building cash reserves include the assurance that, in case of a pay freeze or loss of a job, you can still manage your monthly expenses. The greatest threat to building a cash reserve is the failure to stick to a budget, as well as making a withdrawal from the savings account.

Engage In a Side Job

If your schedule allows, another effective way to build a cash reserve is to engage in a side job. For instance, they are numerous opportunities online that one can work to generate income. The income generated should be saved. Avoid the temptation to use this extra income to sustain the previous lifestyle. Any money made from side jobs should be saved. While engaging in side jobs, take measures to align with your personal budget. A side job should not eat into your budget and it should not exhaust you. Other side jobs that are not online can include teaching at a local club or giving motivational talks.

Managing the Cash Reserve

Now that you have explored ways of enhancing the cash reserve, take time to design ways of setting conditions for access and use of same. For instance, one of the conditions can be that the cash reserve can only be accessed during emergencies, such as a delay in salary payment or a health emergency. The conditions for access can include only one emergency access per month. The withdrawn amount should not be more than a third of the total saved amount.

Considerations

One of the aspects of personal finance that most individuals overlook, concerns donations to charities and extended family support. Even if one does not engage in such activities, it is important to plan and budget for them. In case one does not spend on any of these activities, then the money should be transferred to the savings accounts. The importance of planning for donations to charities as well as extended family support is to minimize items placed under miscellaneous expenditure.

Lastly, after two years, you can start exploring good investment plans. If you are uncertain of engaging in investments that are low risk, then you can leave the cash in the savings account. However, you should consider making a low-risk investment to generate more income. When you make an investment, remember that the returns are the profit and this is what you can use to adjust your financial spending. After a period of time, you will feel the need to adjust your budget upward. The rule is to make sure you are living within your means by using the stated formula of "Living beyond your means=Expenses/Income." If the ratio or percentage is low, all the better. A high ratio or percentage, in this case, means that your expense is more than your income and this is a red flag. You should remember that financial discipline, like any office discipline or school discipline, will take away some of your pleasures, but it is worth the try!

In practice, it is easier to save money but difficult to build a cash reserve. The reason for this flaw is, maintaining the discipline of not withdrawing or using part of the cash reserve is a challenge to most people. It is for this reason that the author suggests you make it difficult to access the bank account where you are building a cash reserve. For instance, the author suggests that you avoid linking the cash reserve bank account with phone withdrawal access or automated teller machine card access. For a start, the author thinks that it will be beneficial to avoid quick access to withdrawing or using the saved cash until you learn financial discipline. Think of a cash reserve as having a fridge full of various foodstuffs, but you have to wait till the agreed time to eat because you are trying to avoid adding weight.

Chapter 5: Habits You Should Change in the Next 24 hours

No matter the size of your bank account, you can model your financial habits on those of the wealthy. Many people assume that millionaires must be free spenders, but for the most part that is not the case. For every rap star or basketball player throwing lavish parties and wasting money foolishly, there are a hundred ordinary millionaires watching their budgets and thinking about the long-term consequences of all the money they spend.

Make a Budget and Stick to It

One of the things most millionaires have in common is the ability to manage their money wisely. It just stands to reason that those who have been able to accumulate a million dollars in assets have learned how to live on less than they earn. Without that basic ability, no amount of income would be sustainable.

Simply put, millionaires are good at creating realistic budgets for their household, and even better at sticking to those spending limits. You can learn from their experience by creating your own household budget and tracking all your expenses.

It may take some time to get your budget right, but once you do, you will be able to see where every dollar is coming from—and where it is going. That ongoing analysis makes it easier to identify opportunities to cut back and find money to invest.

Control Investment Expenses

The ability to control investment expenses is another thing most millionaires have in common. Investment expenses can really eat into your returns, especially over the long term. Since millionaire investors are particularly good at focusing on the long term, they naturally look at the impact of those ongoing expenses.

Wealthy investors also tend to be comfortable making their own investment decisions. They often use discount brokers to buy and sell stocks, saving themselves a lot of money in the process. If you are not ready to invest on your own, paying for an hour or two with a fee-only investment advisor can be a great way to build your portfolio and reduce your risk.

Track Your Accounts but Don't Obsess Over Them

Pay attention to your money. This is big! Tracking investment returns is important, and something that millionaires tend to do quite well. Wealthy investors understand the importance of monitoring their investments and rebalancing their portfolios as needed.

Millionaire investors also understand the difference between monitoring their investments and obsessing over them. They know that the market does not always go up, and they resist the urge to panic when things are bad. Wealthy investors were able to weather the recent financial storm due in part to their discipline and their ability to focus on their long-term goals.

Set Short-Term and Long-Term Financial Goals

One thing wealthy investors have learned to do is set both short-term and long-term financial goals. Knowing the difference between the two makes choosing investments easier and helps investors maintain the discipline that is so important to successful money management.

You can follow their examples by setting attainable short-term goals—like getting out of debt or building an emergency fund. As those parts of your financial life come together, you can start setting long-term goals—like boosting your retirement account or saving for a child's education.

Prioritize Your Savings

Making saving and investing a priority is another common trait of millionaire investors. Those wealthy investors have learned to put their savings first, treating their investment account deposits as just another monthly expense.

You have many ways to follow that valuable example. You can automate your savings simply by signing up for your employer's 401(k) or 403(b) plan. Since the money comes straight out of your paycheck, you do not even have to think about it.

You can also put your savings on automatic by setting up monthly transfers from your bank account to your mutual fund or brokerage account. By treating your investments as just another monthly expense, you learn to live on less than you make while giving your portfolio a kick start.

Prioritize Your Spending

One of the reasons millionaires are able to automate their savings is because they are so good at prioritizing their spending. Wealthy investors have the same kinds of bills as the rest of us, from monthly mortgage payments to health insurance and childcare expenses. What sets them apart is their ability to prioritize their spending and determine which expenses are essential and which are not.

Those wealthy investors are also better than most at distinguishing wants from needs. You might think that the premium cable package or top-shelf cell phone plan is a necessity, but a wealthy investor might look at those things as unnecessary expenses. The ability to prioritize spending and make the most of every dollar is one more thing that separates wealthy investors from the rest of us.

It is tempting to think that every millionaire was born with a silver spoon in their mouth, but that is simply not the case. The vast majority of millionaires are self-made. Understanding what they are doing right and emulating it, is the best way to secure your own financial future.

Chapter 6: Time Management

Time is the most cherished thing that humanity has. Every second that passes, counts, and we hold the complete responsibility to make sure to use every passing second to our maximum benefit. Successful people use their time and energy for time management and gather information and tips to manage time effectively.

Managing time is not all that hard when you look at it on a deeper level. Time can be managed easily by sorting out things that are important and giving them priority in the order of their importance. In this way, you would know your direction before making any plans, and would not waste time and energy unnecessarily.

Now to know, what is time management? How do you go about managing time and what type of information is needed to do so? Time management relates to the set principles of a person and system of decision making based on their consciousness about the tasks that occupy their time.

Having set goals is the most important thing in time management, and without this, it's like walking blindly into a dark room and trying to locate the door for help.

Time management demands a set schedule that works best for you, and in this way you will be able to prioritize your tasks based on the importance and pressing need to finish them in order of priority you set for them. In this way, you will not waste your time beating around the bush.

A lot of people are suffering from this common misconception that doing everything at the same time would reap them more rewards. But these people who multitask usually end up doing nothing tangible or less than what their capabilities are. Greater results can be achieved if tasks are thoughtfully planned out and time is managed properly.

All of us live in a high-paced world today, and there are lots of things we get done in a short span of time—whereas earlier, this was not possible. What we have to look into is, are we getting the maximum benefit out of it or just finishing a task for the sake of finishing it.

We often try to tell ourselves that at least something is done, instead of celebrating that something has been done and accomplished well.

Effective time management will teach you to enjoy your tasks as you derive more pleasure from successfully accomplishing each task. The objective is to set out a realistic time frame for all your daily tasks and gradually become better at doing them. As you become more proficient, you should have more time to spare. Saving time is just like saving money, you must become very organized to do it and identify where time is being wasted. If the task should take an hour, does it take you 1.5 hours—because you became distracted by the internet? Whatever the task is, you must stay focused and get it done in the time allocated. Once you have eliminated time-losing habits, you will derive a sense of satisfaction as you will now be able to get more done with your 24 hours.

Divide your time equally while doing your work and do not leave any room for procrastination. Do not underestimate your ability or overestimate your potential to do a task; observe how much time is required to finish it on time.

Philosophers say that man's main aim in this world is to search for happiness, so our time management should also be based on this factor. Ultimately, it's the feeling of a sense of fulfillment we are looking for only to make us happy and give us the sense of well-being after finishing every task.

We have a very limited time in this world, and we have to do everything at the right time and learn not to postpone things for later, as procrastination is a killer of dreams. It is not possible to do everything in this life, but at the least, we can do most of it by managing our time the right way and do justice to our 24 hours.

We cannot work the whole 24 hours. We need time to sleep and relax. It usually takes 8 hours to have a proper relaxing and reinvigorating sleep.

A lot of people who work need more time. They juggle most of their time between work, travel, childcare, marriage, religious commitments, extended family commitments, entertainment, etc., and have very little time to focus on real financial development, as they do not prioritize tasks correctly.

Whether you are a student, businessperson, model, makeup artist, corporate executive, sales manager, or accountant, time management is imperative for all individuals.

Some companies hold their time management seminars. They buy time management products that can help them train their employees to be more productive. This can also work with you.

There are a lot of time management products that are available on the market now. Time management products can come in different forms like teleseminars or seminars by phone, actual seminars given by spokespersons, video seminars, and books.

There a lot of time management products available on the web that specialize in different areas.

Time management products aim to help us get the most of our daily lives. They aim to make us maximize the time we have every day to attain our ultimate goal.

There are many self-acclaimed or well-known experts on giving time management products. You can easily locate them on the web. Before contacting anyone, make a list first.

With the help of the internet, you can do some checking on what is the best time management product that is available in the market. You can check out their websites, and you might find something that would interest you. So, take a look at those outlined below.

Start with Motivation

Have you ever been to a time management seminar? If you have, you will remember how pumped up you were by the speakers. Do you think it was because they were teaching you some new and improved time management system? Of course not; it is because they motivated the audience into action. Your motivating factor will be the pleasure of getting the things done so that you have the freedom to do what you want.

Write It Down

You must write down what you have to do. This may take the form of a simple to-do list, inputting tasks into a software program or building a spreadsheet. It doesn't matter how you do it, as long as it is easily accessible once it's stored somewhere. You must get it down in writing. The 90% of your current timing problems can be traced back to not getting things out of your head. So keep a written record of everything you need to do.

Accountability

Accountability is the twin sister of the written to-do list. I am not talking about being accountable to some exterior person. No, I am talking about accountability to yourself and your plan to accomplish all that you have to do. To be able to practice effective time management, you have to have something to measure your progress. This should not be an opportunity to beat yourself up. It should be an opportunity to adjust your course, or figure out why you have failed to meet your expectations. Use that information to make fine adjustments and resume course.

Multitasking

If you closely examine the downtime throughout your day, you will find a couple of hours of valuable time lost while commuting, waiting for appointments, or watching TV. How do you find time to read a book or return a phone call? Well, you learn to use these dead times to manage your time effectively. Instead of purchasing a book, get it on CD/Audio and listen to it while commuting to and from work. A book that would take two weeks to read can be 'read' in less than a week if on audio. You can make six 5-minute phone calls while waiting for the doctor. Multitasking during dead time can be a very powerful method to get more done. If you are efficient at time management, you will learn how and when to multitask. The trick is that the main task should not require much concentration, so you can carry out other tasks in that dead time.

Learn to Delegate

If you need to go to the bank and your friend is already going, let him take your deposit to the bank as well. If you have the ability to delegate but do not use it, you are failing to leverage the time properly at your disposal. True, the delegate may not do as good of a job as we would have done, but it does not have to be perfect. It only has to be good enough.

Be More Assertive

You have to learn to say no when others make excessive demands on your time. In many ways, effective time management is a zero-sum game. Every hour you give away decreases your time by one hour while increasing the recipient's by the same amount. The fact is that your time is as valuable, or more valuable than that of other people. Manage your time as you would any other scarce resource. Be assertive and say no.

Every time management system is a house with many rooms. You must learn what motivates you to action and use it to get things done. You must maintain a written record of that which you need to do and check back often to measure your progress. Learn to multitask and delegate so that you get more done each day in the same allotted time. Most importantly, recognize that your time is valuable and should not be given away to others unless they need and deserve it. After all, effective time management is a zero-sum game and every minute you waste or give away is a minute lost forever. Procrastination is very tempting, especially if there is a difficult task. However, putting off tasks or projects is not healthy and prevents a person from becoming productive and living up to their full potential. Learning to overcome procrastination is the key to successful time management.

Chapter 7: Kids and Money

What do you teach your children about money? Whatever it is you teach them will affect their financial future. You can't pass down an education you don't have. If you don't have a financial education, you are increasing the odds that your child will financially struggle.

The cost of buying a home, feeding a family, and sending a child to collage, will rise consistently over the next ten years. The truth is your children will need more money than you in the future.

The rich teach their kids the importance of money. They take their kids to work often. They attend charity events. Over dinner, they explain how businesses fail and succeed. They also talk about stock investments and ownership. These actions and discussions program their children for success.

If you want your son or daughter to enjoy a happy and healthy financial life, fostering a lifelong love of investing can be a smart move. Kids who grow up in money-smart households are more likely to invest their own money wisely when they enter the workforce. Those smart investing decisions can provide many benefits, from a chance at early retirement to fat college funds for their own children.

One of the best ways to create that lifelong love of investing is to choose investments your kids will love. There are many kid-friendly stocks out there, from video game manufacturers to fast food joints and entertainment companies. Making your son or daughter a part owner of these great companies is a terrific way to take the mystery out of investing and make it something exciting.

There are several ways to make your kids part owners in the companies they love. You can buy framed stock certificates for a number of kid-friendly companies—from Disney to McDonald's—and give them as gifts. Those beautifully framed stock certificates make wonderful gifts, and they can become treasured family heirlooms.

Older kids may prefer to invest in their favorite companies directly. If you have a brokerage account already, you can set up a minor account for your child and invest that way. If the account is with a discount broker, the cost of investing can be quite low. There are also direct investment programs like ShareBuilder that allow you to buy shares directly from the companies. Those programs can be quite inexpensive, especially if you invest on an ongoing basis.

No matter how you choose to invest, here are some kid-friendly companies to consider. Chances are these companies are already involved in your child's life, so investing in them allows your son or daughter to share in the success.

1. Walt Disney - even if your child has never been to a Walt Disney World resort, he or she is familiar with the company. From movies and games to TV shows and branded merchandise, the Disney name is everywhere.

2. Hasbro - Hasbro is a big name in toys, and it can be a good choice for your child's investment portfolio as well. You can expect your daughter or son to look at brand names a bit more closely after becoming part owner of the Hasbro Corporation.

3. McDonald's - the golden arches are one of the first things kids learn to recognize, and chances are your own kids have been there a time or two. Your child can enjoy the stock they own every time they enjoy a Happy Meal.

4. Coca Cola and Pepsi - soft drinks are big business, and many kids learn to love these brands early. Even if your son or daughter is not allowed to drink soda, they can share in the future of these ubiquitous brands.

5. Foot Locker - chances are your kids have already chosen their favorite brands of sneakers, and Foot Locker sells most of them. Becoming part owner of this company is a great way to profit from the popularity of those new sneaker styles.

6. Electronic Arts - if your kids love video games, they have probably enjoyed an Electronic Arts release. Give them the gift of Electronic Arts shares and let them share in the fun.

7. Microsoft - Microsoft makes some of the most successful gaming consoles in the world, as well as the operating systems that power their favorite devices. Becoming part owner in this company is a great way to get your kids excited about investing.

Chances are these companies are already involved in your child's life, so investing in them will allow your son or daughter to share in the success.

Chapter 8: Budgeting Goals Accountability

One of the biggest lessons that my past experiences has taught me is that one of the keys to successful habit development is adding accountability for every major goal.

It's not enough to make a personal commitment. The big things in life require a solid action plan and a support network to tap into whenever you encounter an obstacle. This is true for your career trajectory and your personal development. When you have someone to cheer on your successes (or kick you in the butt when you're slacking), you're less likely to give up.

There are a variety of ways to be accountable, like posting your progress on social media accounts or telling the people in your life about your new routine, but we have found that there are three strategies that get the best results.

#1: Self-Accountability

You can create reminders to stick to your budget using calendar alerts or Post-it Notes. You can even put alerts on your phone to remind you when to do particular activities at specific times. These apps and tools are very powerful in helping you add new habits to your daily routine.

You can also use tracking apps for all your habits and hold yourself accountable. I recommend these three in particular:

- StridesApp.com
- Coach.me
- HabitHub

Finally, like we just covered, one of the best tools you can use to stay on top of your finances (and stick to your budget) is to use the YNAB tool.

#2: In-Person Accountability

This is one of the greatest ways to form accountability for budgeting. You have a buddy that you do everything with. In the Navy SEALs, no matter what you do, you have a partner for every single mission. Since you have someone you can rely on, you feel supported and encouraged every step of the way.

The risk of choosing a buddy with the same goal as you is that if one of you stumbles, it can bring the other down also. To avoid this, build a plan for exactly what you're going to do if that buddy falls, so you don't fall with them.

Alternatively, you can have a spouse, personal friend, or an accountability partner—who just checks in to see how your process is going. You can be part of a team or a class, or even reach out to a coach. There are plenty of people who make a living by supporting and encouraging other people on the path to improving their habits and hitting their goals.

#3: Online Accountability

Online accountability is a great way to check in and get quick feedback. We have that within our Facebook group: http://www.HabitsGroup.com.

You can also find online accountability partners and coaches. We've done our best to provide an environment where people can reach out, communicate and give each other online support. If you have questions about shifting your goals or what to do if you stumble, having an online community can make a big difference and help you stay the course.

Be Honest About Your Failures

Sticking to a budget is a war, not a battle. It's a process that you develop over time, not in a moment. This means you will have some slipups and tough days. Even if you fail to track your expenses for a few days, this doesn't mean that you're a failure. Instead, it's a minor hiccup in your journey toward building a positive money habit.

I say all this as a reminder that an accountability buddy is not there to judge you but to support you. That's why it's important to be honest with this person when you have a slipup. This doesn't mean you're a failure. Instead, you're showing a dedication to the accountability process by admitting to those days when you're not sticking to your budget.

Never Break the Chain

The book *The One Thing* tells the story of Jerry Seinfeld's "Don't break the chain" approach that led to his success as a comedian. As the story goes, before Seinfeld became a household name, he made a commitment to write jokes every day. To keep himself accountable, he put a huge annual calendar on his wall and put a red X across every day that he wrote a joke. The goal is to not break the chain.

As Seinfeld said, "Just keep at it and the chain will grow longer every day. You'll like seeing the chain, especially when you get a few weeks under your belt. Your only job is to not break the chain. Don't break the chain."

This can be a very powerful approach for you too. Put a monthly calendar on the wall, and every time you have a success, draw a big X on the day when it's completed. Build a chain of success. You can also use Strides, Coach.me, or HabitHub to track your success; they use the same chain idea.

Our main goal is to recognize that even when we have a day that's less than perfect, we want to maintain that chain of positive action. We don't want to have a complete break. You might have a day where you don't do everything you planned for sticking to a budget. But even if you still spend a few minutes reviewing your budget, then you can consider that a successful day.

Reward Important Milestones

New habits don't have to be boring. Seeing your "chain" getting longer in and of itself can be exciting. On top of that, take the time to celebrate the successful completion of your goals. The reward you pick is up to you, but it's important to celebrate those big moments along the way.

Keep in mind that your reward doesn't have to break the bank. You could check out a new movie, enjoy a night out with your significant other, or simply do something you love.

Again: Just make sure that your reward doesn't conflict with your goal. For example, if your goal is to get out of debt, don't celebrate by going out to a fancy dinner and charging it on your credit card!

Option #1: Create funding goals in YNAB for each of the rewards you plan.

For instance, if you plan to go out to dinner after 21 consecutive days of checking your bank balance, budget the appropriate amount for dinner out so the money's there when you meet that milestone. Monthly funding or target-date goals are especially important for bigger milestones that may include bigger, more expensive rewards. Save consistently, and then enjoy the reward guilt free!

Option #2: Set up a token economy.

In the article "How to Beat Procrastination by Creating a Token Economy," blogger Patrik Edblad shares the following tips for creating a token economy:

- Create specific and measurable daily quotas.

- Get some type of token to reward yourself. For example, poker chips, pennies, beads, or some other random thing you have laying around the house.

- Every time you complete the specific task, put a token into a container.

- Use your tokens to "buy" rewards. For instance, you may reward yourself with dinner out after you have 21 tokens, or splurge on a spa day when you have 90 tokens.

Option #3: Create a visual reminder of your success.

The YouTuber, Homespun Wife, shares about her "Blue Bottle of Happiness" on this video. Every time she and her husband paid off a credit card, they cut it up and put it into a blue, decorative bottle. The bottle is now full of cut up credit cards and serves as a reminder and trophy of their victory over debt.

If you don't have credit card debt but still want a visual reminder of your budgeting habit success journey, you may opt to add a smooth stone, bead, or shiny penny to a clear vase or jar every day you complete a mini habit. Display your "trophy" where you'll see it every day as a reminder of how far you've progressed on your financial journey.

Option #4: Give yourself a talking to.

James Clear often tells himself at the end of a workout, "That was a good day," or, "Good job. You made progress today." If you feel like it, you can tell yourself, "Victory!" or, "Success" each time you do a new habit.

REFLECTION QUESTIONS:

- Which of the three types of accountability (self, online, in person) have you tried? What worked best for you? If you haven't tried any, which type do you feel would work best for you?

- What are some of the biggest challenges you've experienced with accountability?

- How have you personally benefited from accountability?

- Have you ever shared personal information for accountability purposes on a blog or YouTube channel?

- What habit can you realistically do on a daily basis to keep from breaking the chain?

- What visual reminders or rewards will you create to keep your motivation level high?

Select one of the apps mentioned earlier to track the one daily habit you decided to focus on in Step 3. See how long you can go without breaking the chain!

Next, set up either in-person or online accountability. You can join either a budget-specific group or the Develop Good Habits Facebook group, and share your goals so we can hold you accountable.

Create a milestone such as checking your bank balance daily for 30 days, and then come up with a way to celebrate when you reach the milestone. Be sure that the way you decide to celebrate doesn't conflict with your financial goals.

Finally, set up a token system or some other form of visual accountability such as a wall calendar or your own blue bottle of happiness.

Do a Weekly Review

To stay on track and keep small setbacks from becoming deeply ingrained negative habits, plan to spend 20–30 minutes once a week reviewing all your habits and goals. During your weekly review, start by celebrating wins—both big and small.

Next, reflect on any mistakes you've made. Look for patterns to identify obstacles to your success. For instance, upon reflection, you may realize that you blow your budget every time you get together with your sister or a particular friend. Or perhaps you pick up fast food every time your child has a little league baseball game. Or you may also find that the root cause of your setbacks is that you've set too big of a goal.

Third, as you go through the weekly review process, you'll continually find new triggers. Being vigilant and working this plan will help you isolate, analyze, and overcome, so you can either replace those triggers with triggers for positive habits or remove those triggers from your life. If the same mistakes keep happening, ask yourself why. Is the goal too big? Are there other obstacles?

At the end of this weekly review, ask yourself three questions and write down the answers in your journal:

- What went right?
- What went wrong?
- How can I plan for next week?

As an example, every week I check the HabitHub app on my phone for the hard facts about how the week went. I then set a timer and spend 30 minutes freewriting about the events of the week, both good and bad. As I write, I'll often gain clarity about the issues at the root of my struggles. Finally, I'll devise a plan for overcoming those obstacles the next week, and if needed, adjust my goals.

The first actions for this step is to decide what to review weekly, what questions to ask yourself in your review, the tools you'll use for your review, and then what you'll do as a result of the review.

For instance, you may opt to review just your budget in YNAB, ask yourself how you did in your budget that week, and then adapt your budget or your spending plans for the coming week based on what you found in your review.

Or you may choose to use your habit-tracking app such as HabitHub to look at the hard facts when it comes to your consistency, and if things didn't go well, ask yourself what hindered you from doing better and what you need to do in the coming week to up your level of consistency.

Record the answers in Evernote or your journal.

In light of the above, write the following in your journal:

- What habits or goals you'll review weekly
- What questions to ask yourself in the review
- The tools you'll use for your review
- The types of action steps you'll take in the coming week as a result of the review

By the way, be sure to set a time for your weekly review and add it to your calendar. Be committed to the review like you would any other appointment. If something comes up for the same time as your review that you simply must do, rather than skipping the review, schedule it for another time.

Conclusion

The millionaire mindset will ask the question "why should my pay rise or increase in net worth be determined by anyone but me?"

None of us want to be poor, but to generate wealth, we must work hard to reach the goals. However, working hard does not mean you will join the millionaires club. People work hard for decades in low-prospect jobs and still retire broke. You might have come across many stories of millionaires who came from poor backgrounds and became rich. But what has been missing from this narrative is the most important ingredient you can add to hard work – the millionaire mindset.

Anyone can become rich if you learn to think, work and invest like a millionaire. Many self-made millionaires faced the same challenges many of you may currently be facing.

Thank you so much for reading this book!

If you enjoyed this book, then I'd like to ask you for a favor, would you be kind enough to leave a review for this book on Amazon? It'd be greatly appreciated!

Click here to leave a review for this book on Amazon!

Thank you and good luck!

Published by Life Of Opportunity Publishing

www.ingramcontent.com/pod-product-compliance
Lightning Source LLC
Chambersburg PA
CBHW070912220526
45466CB00005B/2193